MARRIAGE ANNULMENT IN THE CATHOLIC CHURCH

by
Stephen Gasche

*All booklets are published thanks to the
generous support of the members of the
Catholic Truth Society*

CATHOLIC TRUTH SOCIETY
PUBLISHERS TO THE HOLY SEE

CONTENTS

The Teaching of the Catholic Church on Marriage 3

The Causes of Marriage Nullity.................................8

   (i) Existence of an Impediment 8

   (ii) Defect of Consent 10

   (iii) Defect of Form...14

Dissolution of a Valid Marriage 16

How the Marriage Annulment Procedure Works 18

Further Reading 21

Notes...23

Stephen Gasche is a former judicial vicar of the diocese of Southwark. He has also lectured in canon law at St John's Seminary, Wonersh.

THE TEACHING OF THE CATHOLIC CHURCH ON MARRIAGE

People often ask what nullity of marriage is all about. Sometimes it is thought of as a Catholic form of divorce. It is also believed by some to be obtainable only by those who are wealthy or influential. Neither of these assertions is true: every person, whether a Catholic or not, has the right to petition for a declaration of nullity of his or her marriage. Such a declaration is quite distinct from a civil divorce; it is rather a declaration by the Catholic Church that a particular union was not a valid marriage. While all who are able to do so are asked to contribute towards the cost of this nullity process, those who are unable to afford it do not have to pay anything at all.[1]

Before discussing what is involved in the marriage nullity process, it is important to understand something of the teaching of the Catholic Church on marriage. For this there is no better starting point than the *Catechism of the Catholic Church*, which offers a succinct description of marriage founded on the teaching of Christ in the Gospels and on the doctrine of the Church: "The matrimonial covenant, by which a man and a woman establish between themselves a partnership of the whole of life, is by its nature ordered toward the good of the spouses and the procreation and education of offspring; this covenant between baptised persons has been raised by Christ the Lord to the dignity of a sacrament."[2]

The Catechism then goes on to express the indissolubility of a valid, sacramental, consummated marriage: "Thus the marriage bond has been established by God himself in such a way that a marriage concluded and consummated between baptised persons can never be dissolved. This bond, which results from the free human act of the spouses and their consummation of the marriage, is a reality, henceforth irrevocable, and gives rise to a covenant guaranteed by God's fidelity. The Church does not have the power to contravene this disposition of divine wisdom."[3]

The Second Vatican Council developed the theology of marriage in its pastoral constitution on the Church in the Modern World, *Gaudium et Spes*. In particular, the Council spoke of marriage as a *covenant* which is brought about by *consent*: "The intimate partnership of life and the love which constitutes the married state has been established by the creator and endowed by him with its own proper laws; it is rooted in the *covenant* of its partners, that is, in their irrevocable personal *consent*."[4] The pastoral constitution then refers to the three traditional Augustinian *goods* of marriage (children, unity and indissolubility), and effectively adds a fourth: the "mutual giving of two persons", referred to in canon 1055§1 of the Code of Canon Law as the "good of the spouses". So we read that: "The intimate union of marriage, as a mutual giving of two persons, and the good of the children demand total fidelity from the spouses and require an unbreakable unity between them."[5]

Pope Paul VI developed the Catholic Church's teaching on marriage in his encyclical *Humanae vitae* on human life. While it is remembered almost exclusively because of its teaching on birth control, it speaks of conjugal love in marriage as being:

- fully *human*, arising from the unity of heart and soul, seeking together to attain their human fulfilment;
- *total*, sharing everything with a love that excludes selfishness and unreasonable exceptions;
- *faithful* and *exclusive* until death;
- *creative of life*, intending to bring new life into being.[6]

The teaching of Paul VI was further developed by a

meeting of the Synod of Bishops in Rome in 1980, which resulted in the Apostolic Exhortation of Pope John Paul II on the Christian Family in the Modern World: *Familiaris Consortio*. In this document Pope John Paul II expanded on the teaching of the Second Vatican Council in *Gaudium et Spes* by writing about the sacramental dignity of marriage between two Christians: "The gift of Jesus Christ is not exhausted in the actual celebration of the sacrament of marriage, but rather accompanies the married couple throughout their lives. This fact is explicitly recalled by the Second Vatican Council when it says that Jesus Christ 'abides with them so that, just as he loved the Church and handed himself over on her behalf, the spouses may love each other with perpetual fidelity through mutual self-bestowal... For this reason, Christian spouses have a special sacrament by which they are fortified and receive a kind of consecration in the duties and dignity of their state. By virtue of this sacrament, as spouses fulfil their conjugal and family obligations, they are penetrated with the Spirit of Christ, who fills their whole lives with faith, hope and charity. Thus they increasingly advance towards their own perfection, as well as towards their mutual sanctification, and hence contribute jointly to the glory of God (*Gaudium et Spes* 48)'."[7]

So if the Catholic Church teaches that marriage is an indissoluble sacrament when it is celebrated between two baptised Christians and consummated, how is it that this same Church can declare such marriages null? The answer is found in the Code of Canon Law[8], the most recent edition of which was promulgated in 1983, which expresses the teaching of the Catholic Church on marriage in a juridical form. There are found the laws - known as 'canons' - which set out all the requirements for marriage in both divine law and church law. So in order to enter this marriage covenant validly the parties concerned must be free from any impediment (canons 1083-1094), must exchange proper consent (canons 1095-1103), and must - if one or both of them are Catholic - do so according to canonical form (canons 1108-1127). We must therefore look now at the causes of marriage nullity, in order to understand the reasons for which the Catholic Church declares marriage null.

THE CAUSES OF MARRIAGE NULLITY

(i) Existence of an Impediment

There are two impediments to marriage which are of natural law and so affect all who may wish to marry. The first is the impediment of impotence, but such a restriction applies only if the impotence is antecedent to the marriage and is perpetual. If there is any doubt about the alleged impotence the marriage is not to be impeded, and sterility neither inhibits nor invalidates marriage. The second is the existence of a previous bond of marriage. This impediment means that someone who is divorced may not remarry in the Catholic Church until and unless their first union is either declared null or dissolved by the Church. The Catholic Church does not recognise divorce as having anything other than civil effects.

With the exception of some of the impediments of consanguinity and affinity, all the other impediments are of ecclesiastical (i.e. Catholic Church) law, and so bind only Catholics and those who wish to marry Catholics.

So, for example, a marriage would be invalid if it were

entered by those who were below the minimum age for marriage: 16 for men and 14 for women in canon law - although in practice the Church follows the civil law minimum age of 16 for both. It is also invalid when it takes place between a Catholic and an unbaptised person without a dispensation; or when it is entered by a Catholic deacon, priest or bishop without being dispensed from the obligation of celibacy; or by a religious brother or sister without obtaining an indult to leave the religious institute.

There are several other impediments to marriage, the most significant of which are those of consanguinity and affinity, i.e. a relationship by blood or by marriage respectively. These rules are necessarily complicated, but the simplest way to remember them is that if two people who are first cousins wish to marry they need a dispensation from the impediment of consanguinity. Any relationship more distant than this does not impede marriage.

So if there is an impediment to a marriage that has not been dispensed, the Catholic Church may declare that union null because it was entered into invalidly by reason of either divine or ecclesiastical law. But surely most impediments to marriage are usually dispensed anyway when Catholics enter marriage in the Catholic Church? Yes, they are, so it is relatively rare for the Church to declare marriages null due to an impediment which has not been dispensed. We therefore have to turn to the more usual headings of nullity, and these refer to the consent which the parties to a marriage must exchange in order to marry validly.

(ii) Defect of Consent

When a couple exchange their consent to "a partnership of the whole of life"[9], they require the *capacity* for marriage, the *knowledge* of what marriage is, and the *will* to enter marriage. So if one or both of the parties lacks the capacity for marriage, or lacks knowledge of marriage, or does not intend to enter marriage, the consent is invalid. For example, two of the more commonly used headings of nullity are used in cases where someone has lacked the capacity for marriage. One of these refers to those who have a "grave lack of discretion of judgment concerning the rights and obligations of marriage which are to be mutually given and accepted" (canon 1095°2).

So if someone entered marriage because of pressure due to pregnancy, or in order to escape from the parental home, or on the rebound from a previous relationship, or while under the influence of alcohol or drugs, or because he or she was too young to make such a life-long commitment, the marriage tribunal may find sufficient evidence to prove that such a person was gravely lacking in the judgment required to enter marriage.

The second of these headings applies to those "who are not capable of assuming the essential obligations of marriage due to causes of a psychological nature" (canon 1095°3). Here evidence would be required to show, for example, that someone was incapable of entering marriage due to a particular psychological condition. In such cases expert opinion may be sought in order to assist the tribunal in its judgment.

It may be, however, that someone had the capacity for marriage but was lacking in knowledge of marriage. This does not mean simply a lack of knowledge of marriage itself - although such a person would enter marriage invalidly if his or her *erroneous* opinion of what marriage is determined the will (canon 1099). Rather it concerns the particular person someone wishes to marry. For example, if a specific quality of the other spouse was principally intended - such as the other spouse being a Catholic - and someone married that spouse in error concerning that fact, the consent would be invalid. Likewise someone who marries the wrong person - such as the bride's twin sister - does so invalidly! (canon 1097). Perhaps a person may enter marriage deceived by fraud concerning some quality of the other party which of its very nature could seriously disturb their married life. Were such deceit fraudulently perpetrated in order to obtain consent (canon 1098), such consent would be invalid.

Sometimes a person entering marriage is quite capable of doing so, and has full knowledge of what marriage is and of the essential qualities of the person he or she wishes to marry, but positively wills either to exclude marriage itself or some essential element or property of marriage (canon 1101§2). The presumption about marriage is, of course, that the parties intend and mean what they say when they exchange consent, but there are occasions when, for example, someone will enter marriage solely to obtain a visa or to fulfil a residency requirement. Such consent would be invalid because marriage itself would have been excluded by a positive act of the will.

Perhaps someone may enter marriage intending the partnership to be just for the good of himself or herself rather than for the good of both the spouses, or intending to permanently exclude children from the whole life of the marriage, or intending to be unfaithful, or with the intention that the marriage could end in divorce if it did not work out. In any of these cases the consent would be invalid if the tribunal could prove that one or both parties to the marriage entered it with such an act of the will. It is also possible for someone to enter marriage with a condition concerning the future of the marriage (canon 1102), or due to force or grave fear (canon 1103). Such consent would also be invalid, because in order to enter marriage validly one must do so with complete freedom and without any duress.

In all these instances of invalid consent to marriage, the tribunal must obtain evidence in order that it can be morally certain that the consent furnished at the time of the marriage was indeed invalid - either due to a lack of capacity to enter marriage, or due to a lack of knowledge concerning the essence of marriage or the principal qualities of the other spouse, or due to a positive act of the will which intended to exclude either marriage itself or some essential element or property of marriage. It is under these headings of nullity that the Catholic Church declares marriages null, but only after a thorough process which gives both parties and their witnesses the right to participate in the nullity procedure.

(iii) Defect of Form

There is another reason why the Church declares that a person who has already been married and is now divorced is free to marry. This is by reason of defect of form. This is because the Church requires its members to exchange their consent generally before a Catholic priest or deacon, in accordance with the Catholic rite of marriage, and in the presence of two witnesses. If a Catholic enters a marriage without this form being observed - and without a dispensation - he or she does so invalidly. Thus a civil marriage where one or both of the parties are Catholic, whether celebrated in a non-Catholic church or in a register office, may be declared null due to a lack of canonical form, enabling each of the parties to enter a new marriage (canons 1108, 1117). It may also be that a visiting priest or deacon celebrating the marriage was not duly delegated, or that there were not two witnesses present. In such cases a marriage may also be declared null.

It is not uncommon, however, when in a mixed marriage the non-Catholic is a committed member of his or her Christian church, for the couple to request a dispensation from the canonical form of marriage in order that they may validly marry in that non-Catholic church. Such a dispensation is granted by a local ordinary of the diocese in these circumstances, so that the couple's marriage is recognised by the Catholic Church (canon 1127§2).

One of the most frequent questions asked by people who approach the Catholic Church with a view to obtaining a declaration of nullity is what effect it would have on the legitimacy of their children. The answer is that, in those cases where the nullity is proven on the basis of the existence of an impediment or due to defect of consent, the children are still regarded by the Church as legitimate. The reason for this is that they are regarded as being born of a putative or supposed marriage, which at least one of the parties celebrated in good faith.

DISSOLUTION OF A VALID MARRIAGE

We saw earlier that the Catholic Church teaches that a valid, sacramental and consummated marriage cannot be dissolved by any human power for any reason other than death (canon 1141). So how is it that the Church can dissolve certain marriages? Surely this would contradict the Church's own teaching? The reason is that although a marriage may be valid, it is only a sacrament when it is celebrated between two baptised Christians, So a marriage entered into by two people, one or both of whom are not baptised, is called a natural bond of marriage. It is presumed - as are all marriages - to be valid unless the contrary is proven, but in certain circumstances it may be dissolved 'in favour of the faith' of the Christian party. The origins of such a dissolution are found in St Paul's first letter to the Corinthians: "If the unbeliever wishes to separate, however, let him do so. The believing husband or wife is not bound in such cases. God has called you to live in peace" (1 *Cor* 7:15). The Pauline Privilege may be granted only when there is a marriage of two unbaptised people and one of them wishes to convert to Christianity. Then, either if the non-baptised party refuses to live in peace with the convert without insult to the Creator, or if the non-baptised person departs the marital home even without the convert being the cause, the new Christian may enter a new marriage. The previous bond of marriage is dissolved by virtue of the Pauline Privilege at the moment the new marriage is entered. (canons 1143 - 1147).

Since 1924 all the Popes, by virtue of their Petrine office, have extended the principle of the Pauline Privilege to embrace other types of non-sacramental marriages, whether between two unbaptised people or between a Christian and an unbaptised person. In these cases, however, the application for a dissolution by virtue of the Petrine Privilege - as it is known - has to be sent by the diocese to Rome, and this privilege is allowed by the Pope himself.[10]

The other occasion on which a marriage may be dissolved is when it has not been consummated. Such situations are in fact very rare, but when they do arise it is possible for a case to be prepared and sent to Rome. Again it is the Pope who grants a dissolution of a valid but non-consummated marriage, whether it is a sacrament or not (canon 1142).

How the Marriage Annulment Procedure Works

So what is involved in making an application for a declaration of nullity? The first step is for the person applying for the nullity, known as the petitioner or plaintiff, to contact a Catholic priest. This might be a priest of the parish of either of the parties to the marriage, or another priest known to one of them. He will normally supply a form to complete, which enables the petitioner to set out the basic facts of the marriage. This is then sent to the diocesan marriage tribunal, where the case will either be examined or sent on to another tribunal which has competence according to Church law.

If the case is accepted for judgment, it is assigned to someone known as an instructing judge. The judge - a priest, deacon or lay person - interviews the petitioner and, if he or she is willing to take part in the nullity process, the other party to the marriage, known as the respondent. It is important to note that the respondent has a right to take part in the process, but should he or she decline to exercise this right the case can still proceed. Both parties may nominate witnesses: family and friends who knew them before or at the time of the marriage. The witnesses are usually interviewed by one of a team of lay auditors, who gather evidence for the case. Sometimes an advocate is assigned to argue the case for the petitioner, or to represent the interests of the respondent.

When all the evidence is available the case is examined by someone called the defender of the bond. It is his or her responsibility to defend the bond of marriage and to argue the case against a decree of nullity being proven. After the case has been to the defender, it normally goes to a panel of three judges who meet to make a judgment as to whether the alleged nullity of marriage is proven or not proven. This judgment of the marriage, carefully evaluating and judging the statements of the petitioner and respondent, the evidence of the witnesses, the arguments of the advocate if one has been used, and the observations of the defender of the bond, brings to a conclusion the 'first instance' part of the nullity process.

If the decision is in favour of nullity, the case is automatically referred to an appeal Court, usually a Marriage Tribunal of another Diocese. If the appeal court agrees with the first instance court that the nullity of a marriage has been proven, a decree of nullity is issued and both parties are free to marry. If the first instance decision is in the negative (i.e. against nullity) the petitioner has the right to appeal to the second instance court. If first instance and appeal courts judge that the nullity has not been proven, the marriage must be assumed to be valid and so the parties are not free to enter a new union. It is only when there is a different outcome between the two courts that the petitioner has the right to appeal to the Roman Rota, which is the tribunal in Rome where the final adjudication of the union takes place.[11]

So the Catholic Church does declare marriages null when it is proved with moral certainty that a particular union was entered either with an impediment, or without valid consent, or without canonical form. The essential purpose of the diocesan marriage tribunal is to offer help to people who, for whatever reason, find themselves in difficult marriage situations. While always remaining faithful to the principle that every valid, sacramental, consummated marriage is indissoluble, the marriage tribunals of the Church are always ready to investigate an alleged claim of nullity in order that one of Christ's faithful may be declared free to marry another who is similarly free. It is in this way that marriage annulment in the Catholic Church can offer a truly pastoral solution to the many people who turn to the Church for help, so that they may once again lead full sacramental lives as members of the people of God.

FURTHER READING

BROWN, Ralph, Marriage Annulment in the Catholic Church, (third edition), published by Kevin Mayhew Ltd, Bury St Edmunds, 1990.

CATECHISM OF THE CATHOLIC CHURCH, *Libreria Editrice Vaticana*, 1992; United Kingdom version of English-language translation, published by Geoffrey Chapman, London, 1994.

DOOGAN, H,(ed.) Catholic Tribunals: Marriage Annulment and Dissolution, published by E J Dwyer, Newtown, New South Wales, Australia, 1990.

FLANNERY, A, (ed.) Vatican Council II: The Conciliar & Post-Conciliar Documents, Study Edition, New York, 1987.

JOHN PAUL II, *Familiaris consortio*, 1981, in *Acta Apostolicae Sedis*, vol. LXXIV, 1982, pp. 82-191. English language edition, Catholic Truth Society, London, 1981.

PAUL VI, *Humanae vitae*, in *Acta Apostlicae Sedis*, vol. LX, 1968. English language, revised edition, Catholic Truth Society, London.

THE CANON LAW: Letter & Spirit, Canon Law Society of Great Britain & Ireland, published by Geoffrey Chapman, London, 1995.

NOTES

1 Extract from article published in Southwark diocesan magazine, *Outreach*, December 1997, reproduced by kind permission of the editor

2 *Catechism of the Catholic Church*, 1601

3 *Ibid.*, 1640

4 *Gaudium et Spes*, 48

5 *Ibid.*, 48

6 *Humanae vitae*, 9

7 *Familiaris consortio*, 56

8 *Codex iuris canonici auctoritate Ioannis Pauli PP. II promulgatus*, Libreria Editrice Vaticana, 1983, xxx, p 317. American version of English-language translation: Code of Canon Law, Latin-English ed., translation prepared under the auspices of the Canon Law Society Of America, Washington DC, 1983, xlii

9 *Gaudium et Spes*, 48

10 *Ut notum est*, instruction and procedure for the dissolution of marriage in favour of the faith, 1973

11 Extract from article in *Outreach*, *op. cit.*

Informative Catholic Reading

We hope that you have enjoyed reading this booklet.

If you would like to find out more about CTS booklets - we'll send you our free information pack and catalogue.

Please send us your details:

Name ....

Address ....

....

....

Postcode ....

Telephone...

Email ....

Send to: CTS, 40-46 Harleyford Road,
                   Vauxhall, London
                   SE11 5AY

Tel: 020 7640 0042
Fax: 020 7640 0046
Email: info@cts-online.org.uk